The Official

 **IRB RUGBY WORLD CUP 2015**

ACTIVITY
BOOK

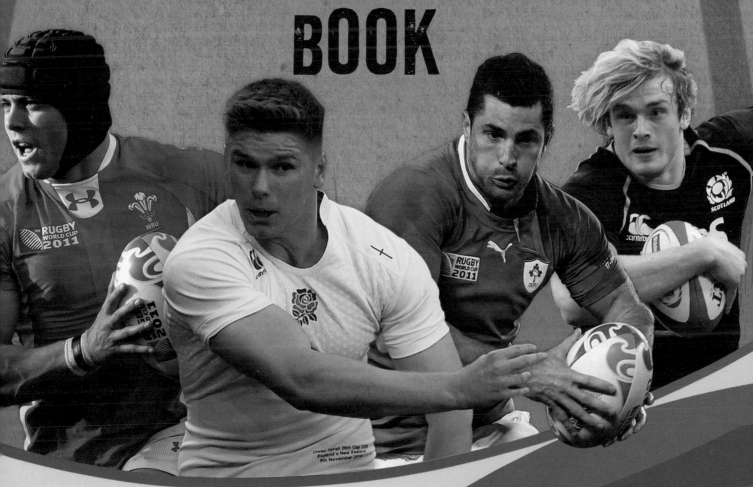

Contents

Published in 2015

TM © Rugby World Cup Limited 1986

Produced under licence by Carlton Books Ltd
An imprint of the Carlton Publishing Group
20 Mortimer Street, London W1T 3JW

Text, design and illustration © Carlton Books Limited 2015

Author and Editor: Tasha Percy
Design Manager: Emily Clarke
Designer: Andy Jones
Consultant: Clive Gifford
Production: Marion Storz

10 9 8 7 6 5 4 3 2 1

ISBN: 978-1-78312-123-6

Printed in China

PICTURE CREDITS
The publishers would like to thank the following sources for their kind permission to reproduce the pictures in this book.

Getty Images: /Shaun Botterill: 12-13, 21, 25; /Gabriel Bouys/AFP: 8CL; /Jean Catuffe: 17; /Franck Fife/AFP: 22, 38B; /Stu Forster: 8L, 8R, 32T; /Matt King: 46; /Mark Kolbe: 27, 32C; /Jan Kruger: 38T; /Warren Little: 28-29; /Alex Livesey: 33C; /Philippe Lopez/AFP: 8BR, 18, 33L, 43; /Mark Metcalfe: 4; /Sandra Mu: 16, 24, 47; /MyLoupe/Universal Images Group: 37; /Hannah Peters: 8TC, 8TR, 35B; /Ryan Pierse: 39T; /David Rogers: 8BL, 19, 20, 34T, 34B, 39B; /Christophe Simon/AFP: 33R; /Cameron Spencer: 33B; /Mark Thompson: 35T, 53BL; /William West/AFP: 32B; /Greg Wood/AFP: 8CR

Press Association Images: /David Davies: 53BR; /Christophe Ena/AP: 48-49; /Alastair Grant/AP: 48L

Every effort has been made to acknowledge correctly and contact the source and/or copyright holder of each picture and Carlton Books Limited apologizes for any unintentional errors or omissions that will be corrected in future editions of this book.

Time keeping

A rugby match is 80 minutes in total. It is split into two halves of 40 minutes each, with a half time of between 10 and 15 minutes.

Can you draw on the clock where the hands should be at different points of the match?

If the match started at 2.30pm, what time would it be...

a) 15 minutes in?

b) at the start of half time?

c) half way through the second half (with a 15-minute break)?

d) five minutes before the end of the match (with a 15-minute break)?

Spectacular stadiums

England is hosting Rugby World Cup 2015. Thirteen stadiums across eleven cities will host matches. Twelve of the stadiums are in England and one is in Wales. Stick the stadiums in the correct boxes next to the map. Can you fill in the name and location for each one?

Stadium : ....

Location: ....

Stadium : ....

Location: ....

Stadium : ....

Location: ....

Stadium : ....

Location: ....

Stadium : ....

Location: ....

Stadium : ....

Location: ....

6

Stadium : ....

Location: ....

7

Stadium : ....

Location: ....

8

Stadium : ....

Location: ....

Stadium : ....

Location: ....

Stadium : ....

Location: ....

Stadium : ....

Location: ....

Stadium : ....

Location: ....

13

Pitch perfect

Answers on page 56.

Below is the outline of a rugby pitch and markings for all the different lines. A pitch is split into two halves. Colour in the pitch and fill in the missing markings.

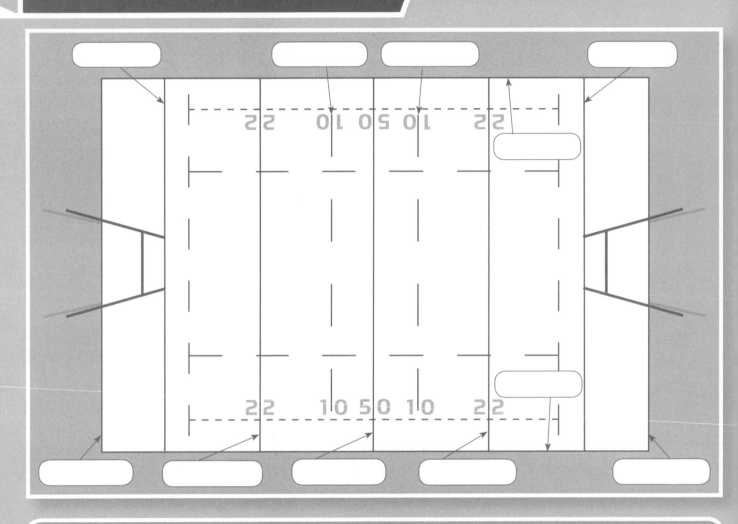

FACT CARD 2
What's with all the lines?

Each line marks out a different area of the pitch.

- **Half-way line:** This line marks the centre of the pitch. Each team must defend their own half as well as attacking their opponent's half. Teams swap halves at half time.
- **10-metre line:** This line marks a 10-metre distance from the half-way line. When a kick-off happens, to start the game, the ball must travel further than this line. If it doesn't the opposition will be given a scrum at the centre of the half-way line and they throw in the ball.

- **22-metre line:** This line marks a distance of 22 metres from the goal line.
- **Goal line:** This marks the line that a player must reach or cross to touch down the ball and score a try. The goalposts are positioned half way along the goal line.
- **Dead-ball line:** This line marks the end of the pitch. Once the ball crosses this line it is out of play.
- **Touchline:** This line runs the length of the pitch on both sides. If the ball crosses this line it is out of play.

 Answers on page 56.

Player positions

There are fifteen players on a team, made up of eight forwards and seven backs. Each position has its own job to do but generally forwards are bigger and stronger and backs are smaller and faster. Using your stickers, place the numbered shirts on the correct positions.

Forwards:
1. Loose-head prop
2. Hooker
3. Tight-head prop
4. Lock or second row
5. Lock or second row
6. Blind-side flanker
7. Open-side flanker
8. Number 8

Backs:
9. Scrum-half
10. Fly-half
11. Left wing
12. Inside centre
13. Outside centre
14. Right wing
15. Full-back

Answers on page 56.

Who? Where?

RUGBY WORLD CUP 2015

Can you match these rugby players to their shirts. See if you can guess which country they play for. Can you remember the names for the different positions?

Name: Thierry Dusautoir

Country:...................

Name: Will Genia

Country:...................

Name: Richie Gray

Country:...................

Name: Dan Carter

Country:...................

Name: Rob Kearney

Country:...................

Name: Adam Jones

Country:...................

Name: Dylan Hartley

Country:...................

Name: Bryan Habana

Country:...................

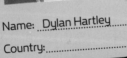

Colourful kit

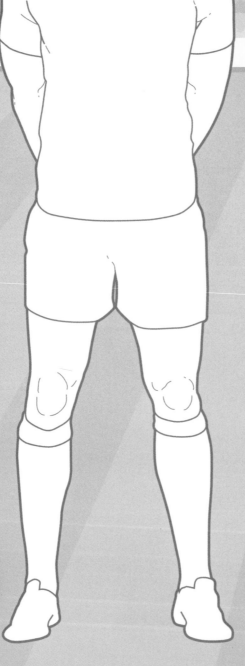

A rugby kit is made up of a shirt, shorts, socks and rugby boots. All teams have a primary kit and an alternative kit. The away team wears the primary kit in the event of a clash to avoid confusion on the pitch. Can you colour in the kits in different colours?

10

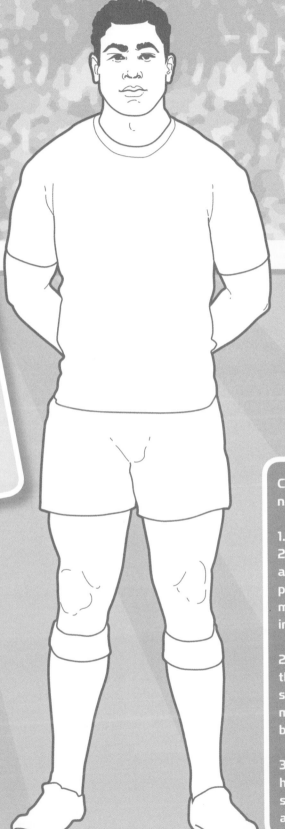

FACT CARD 3

Changing colours

England's primary kit is currently a short-sleeved white shirt with a red rose emblem, white shorts and navy socks with a white top. Their alternative kit has changed a lot over the years and some of the colours have included black, red, navy and purple.

Can you work out these number puzzles?

1. If each team in RWC 2015 has two kits for all of their players (30 players in total) how many shirts are there in total?

2. What if a quarter of the teams use the same socks for both kits. How many socks would there be in total?

3. If only half the teams have two different shorts, how many shorts are there in total?

Kick-off!

This is a picture of the start of a match. Argentina are about to kick off.
All players on the kicker's team must be standing behind the kicker and ready to chase down the ball. Add a sticker for where you would place the referee.

FACT CARD 4

Referee tasks

A referee has three main tasks that he must perform during a match:

1. To make sure the game is being played by the laws.
2. To decide if tries have been scored and who should get the ball when it leaves the pitch.
3. To keep track of the time and score.

Do you think you could be a referee?

Answer on page 56.

Rugby match-up

See how many rugby items you can recognise.
Draw a line to match the rugby image with
the correct name.

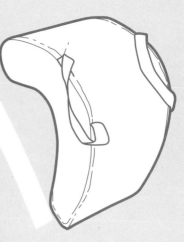

goalposts

tackle bag

scrumcap

kicking tee

rucking shield

gumshield

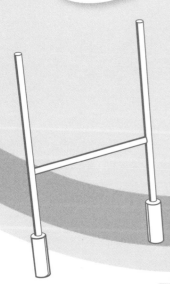

Scoring big

To win a match a team must score more points than their opponents. There are three ways a team can score points:

- A try is scored when a player touches the ball down on or behind the opposition's goal line. The closer the ball is placed to the goal posts, the easier the conversion kick will be. The referee can also award a penalty try.

  A try is worth 5 points.

- A conversion is awarded after a try. A player will have a chance to kick the ball through the goalposts.

  A conversion is worth 2 points.

- A goal kick can be either a drop goal or a penalty kick through the goalposts. A drop goal is when a player releases the ball from their hands and kicks it after it has bounced on the ground. A penalty kick is awarded by the referee if there has been foul play, and is usually taken from a kicking tee.

  Both goal kicks are worth 3 points.

Can you work out how many points each of these teams have scored:

1. 2 tries + 2 conversion + 1 penalty kick =
2. 5 tries + 3 conversions + 0 penalty kicks =
3. 7 tries + 6 conversions + 0 penalty kicks =
4. 1 try + 1 conversion + 8 penalty kicks =
5. 4 tries + 4 conversions + 6 penalty kicks =

Are any of these scores the same?

Which score is the highest?

Super scrum

Can you guess where the ball is in the scrum? Place a rugby ball sticker in the square where you think it should be.

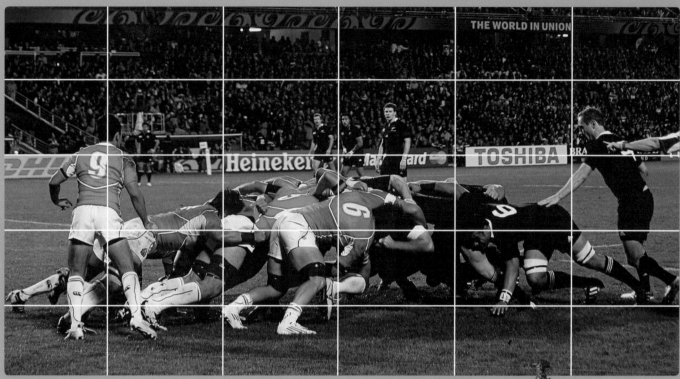

A scrum involves all eight of the forwards of both teams. Here is how a scrum should be performed:

1. Teammates bind in three rows and crouch down ready. The front row interlock heads with their opponents.

2. When the two teams are interlocked a space called a tunnel is formed between the front row of each team.

3. The scrum-half must throw the ball into this tunnel. The forwards try to gain and maintain possession of the ball, using their feet.

4. The team that wins the ball can either try and move forwards with it or roll it back to the number 8, where the scrum-half can pick it up and pass it to the backs.

Puzzling pattern

Look carefully at the rugby picture patterns. Can you find the stickers that should come next in each row?

1.

2.

3.

4.

5.

Answers on page 56.

Quiz: Laws of the game

Ready to test your knowledge of the laws of rugby?
See how many of these questions you can answer.
Circle the answer you think is correct – remember only one is right.

1. To start the game:
a) The ball must be kicked forwards.
b) The ball must travel more than 10 metres forwards.
c) All the other players must stand behind the kicker.
d) All of the above.

2. When passing the ball:
a) The ball can only be passed forwards.
b) The player must only pass to the player next to them.
c) The ball must only be passed level or backwards.
d) The ball can be thrown in any direction.

3. Tackles must be made:
a) Above the knee.
b) Below the shoulder.
c) From in front.
d) All of the above.

4. Once a player has been tackled to the ground:
a) The tackler must roll away and the tackled player must release the ball.
b) The tackler must roll away and the tackled player can get up and continue playing.
c) The tackler can try to get hold of the ball and the other player must release the ball.
d) Neither player should do anything until their team members have arrived.

5. To create a ruck:
a) Players in the ruck must be on their feet.
b) Two players on opposing teams must be in physical contact.
c) The ball must be on the ground.
d) All of the above.

6. In a lineout:

a) A player can push opponents out of the way to try and get the ball.

b) Teammates can pre-grip a player to lift them to catch the ball.

c) A player can be lifted by his teammates before the ball has been thrown in.

d) The player throwing in the ball is allowed to throw direct to their team.

7. In a maul:

a) All players involved must be on their feet and bound together.

b) A minimum of three players must be involved – one with the ball and a teammate who is driving him forwards as well as a member of the opposition.

c) If it stops moving twice, the ball must be played immediately.

d) All of the above.

8. A try is scored when:

a) The ball is kicked over the goal line and lands before the dead-ball line, but doesn't go through the goalposts.

b) The player throws the ball downwards once they have crossed the goal line.

c) The player pushes down on the ball with the upper part of their body past the goal line.

d) A player carrying the ball has run across the goal line without dropping the ball or being tackled.

9. A player is offside:

a) If they are in front of a teammate carrying or kicking the ball.

b) If they join a ruck or maul from the side.

c) If they are not taking part in a lineout but are standing less than 10 metres from the lineout.

d) All of the above.

10. To make a mark:

a) The player must be behind his own 22-metre line when he catches the ball and shouts "mark".

b) The player must catch the ball in the air and land with both feet on the ground at the same time.

c) The ball may bounce once before the player catches it.

d) All of the above.

Answers on page 56.

Courageous captains

Chris Robshaw has been England's captain since 2012 and Sergio Parisse has captained the Italian team since 2008. The six images of these brave captains may look very similar but they are all slightly different to the original, except for one. Can you circle the image that matches the original exactly?

Chris Robshaw

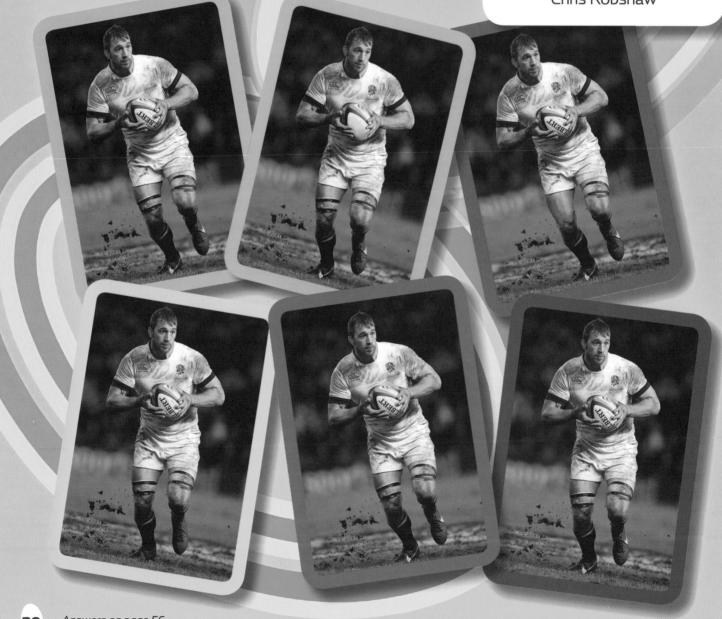

Answers on page 56.

Sergio Parisse

Quiz: True or false

Time to test how much you really know. Can you work out which of these situations would lead to a penalty being awarded by the referee? Answer true or false and whether you think a penalty would be awarded or not.

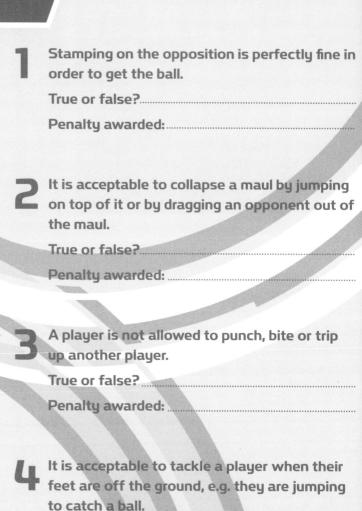

1 Stamping on the opposition is perfectly fine in order to get the ball.

True or false?..

Penalty awarded:...

2 It is acceptable to collapse a maul by jumping on top of it or by dragging an opponent out of the maul.

True or false?..

Penalty awarded:...

3 A player is not allowed to punch, bite or trip up another player.

True or false?..

Penalty awarded:...

4 It is acceptable to tackle a player when their feet are off the ground, e.g. they are jumping to catch a ball.

True or false?..

Penalty awarded:...

5 If a player charges down the ball as an opponent kicks it and makes contact with the ball, this is a knock-on.

True or false?..

Penalty awarded:...

6 Intentionally blocking a teammate with the ball so that the opposition cannot tackle them is a form of obstruction.

True or false? ....

Penalty awarded: ....

7 A player can intentionally knock the ball forwards using their arm or hands, as long as they don't pass it forwards.

True or false? ....

Penalty awarded: ....

8 It is okay to charge down a player after they have kicked the ball.

True or false? ....

Penalty awarded: ....

9 During a lineout the player has to throw the ball straight between the two teams.

True or false? ....

Penalty awarded: ....

10 Tackling a player without the ball is considered dangerous play.

True or false? ....

Penalty awarded: ....

Answers on page 56.

Moving forwards

Can you complete the jigsaws to see what is missing? One scene is of a scrum and the other is a lineout. Find the stickers to complete each puzzle. Then write whether it is a scrum or a lineout.

This is a ....

Answers on page 56.

This is a _____

Answers on page 56.

FACT CARD 4
Scrum vs. Lineout

- Both of these set pieces are performed by the forwards.

- The scrum includes all eight forwards, but a lineout can contain between three and eight forwards.

- A scrum is awarded when the ball has gone forwards or been knocked on, the ball has not come out of a ruck or maul, or because a player or players were accidentally offside.

- A lineout is awarded if the ball has gone out of play, either from being kicked, thrown or knocked out.

The Draw

The Draw was made in London on December 3, 2012. Twelve countries qualified directly after finishing in the top three of their respective pools at RWC 2011. The other eight teams were determined by a global qualification process and were represented in the draw by the title of their relevant region (e.g. Oceania 1) or the repechage winner. There are four pools of five teams. Only two teams will make it out of each pool into the quarter-finals. Can you fill in the missing countries that have qualified for RWC 2015?

POOL A

Australia

England

Wales

?

?

POOL B

South Africa

Samoa

Scotland

?

?

RUGBY WORLD CUP 2015

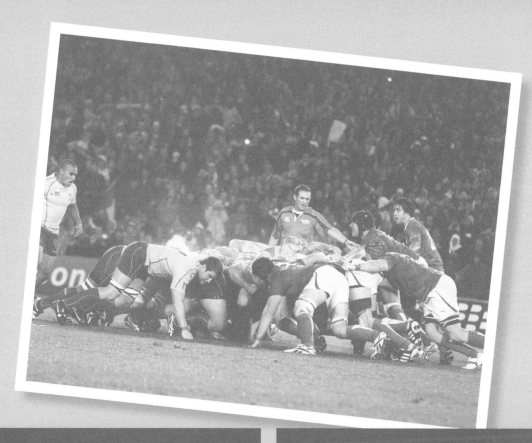

POOL C

New Zealand

Argentina

Tonga

?

?

POOL D

France

Ireland

Italy

?

?

Answers on page 56.

Yellow card!

When a player has acted recklessly, either by making a dangerous tackle or another form of foul play, the referee may give them a yellow card. The player must sit in the sin bin on the sidelines for 10 minutes, leaving his team with one less player during this time.

Can you spot ten differences between the two images of a player being given a yellow card during Rugby World Cup 2011?

1 **2** **3** **4** **5**

6 **7** **8** **9** **10**

Match the ten numbers to the ten differences. One has been done for you.

Magic moment

Just before the start of a match the two teams form a straight line facing towards one side of the crowd. They both sing their national anthem before the game begins. This is a magical moment for the crowd and their team to unite in their passion for rugby. Can you colour in the team line-up? Make sure all the players' kits are the same colour.

Can you match up the national anthems or ceremonial dances with the right country?

National anthems	
England	The Star Spangled Banner
Scotland	Hen Wlad Fy Nhadau
Wales	Kimigayo
Japan	La Marseillaise
USA	Flower of Scotland
France	God Save the Queen

Ceremonial dances	
New Zealand	The Siva Tau
Tonga	The Cibi/Bola
Samoa	The Sipi Tau
Fiji	The Haka

Answers on page 56.

It's game time!

4 — Whoops! You threw a forwards pass, go back a space.

5

12

3

6 — You score a drop goal. Advance 3 spaces.

11

2

7

10 — Your team gets a scrum. If you roll an even number, go forwards 2 spaces. If not, go back 2 spaces.

1 — KICK OFF

8 — The referee catches you offside. Go back a space.

9

How to Play:

- Grab a dice and some friends or family members to compete against.
- Make your rugby counters by attaching your rugby stickers to some card.
- Starting with the youngest, take it in turns to roll the dice and move your counters along the board.
- Follow the instructions in the square you land on.
- You must throw the exact number to land on the last square.
- The first player to the end will win Rugby World Cup and get to lift the Webb Ellis Cup.

13

Congratulations! You've scored a try. Advance 5 spaces

20

21

14

19

Well done, you made a conversion. Advance 2 spaces.

22

Oh no, knock-on. Go back a space.

15

18

23

16

You make an illegal high tackle. Miss your next 2 turns.

17

24

FINISH!
You've won!

Record-breakers crossword

Can you guess the record-breaking rugby players' names? There are clues to help you. Fill in the players' full names on the crossword.

Clues

Across

1. IRB Player of the Year for 2011.
   Country: France

2. Captain of the winning team, RWC 2007.
   Country: South Africa

3. IRB Player of the Year for 2008.
   Country: Wales

4. Most drop goals in a RWC tournament.
   Country: England

5. Most appearances at RWC.
   Country: England

Down

1. IRB Player of the Year for 2013.
   Country: New Zealand

2. Most conversions in one tournament, RWC 1987.
   Country: New Zealand

3. Most tries in a match by a player, RWC 1995.
   Country: New Zealand

4. Most drop goals in a match, RWC 1999.
   Country: South Africa

5. Youngest player to appear at RWC.
   Country: USA

Twickenham

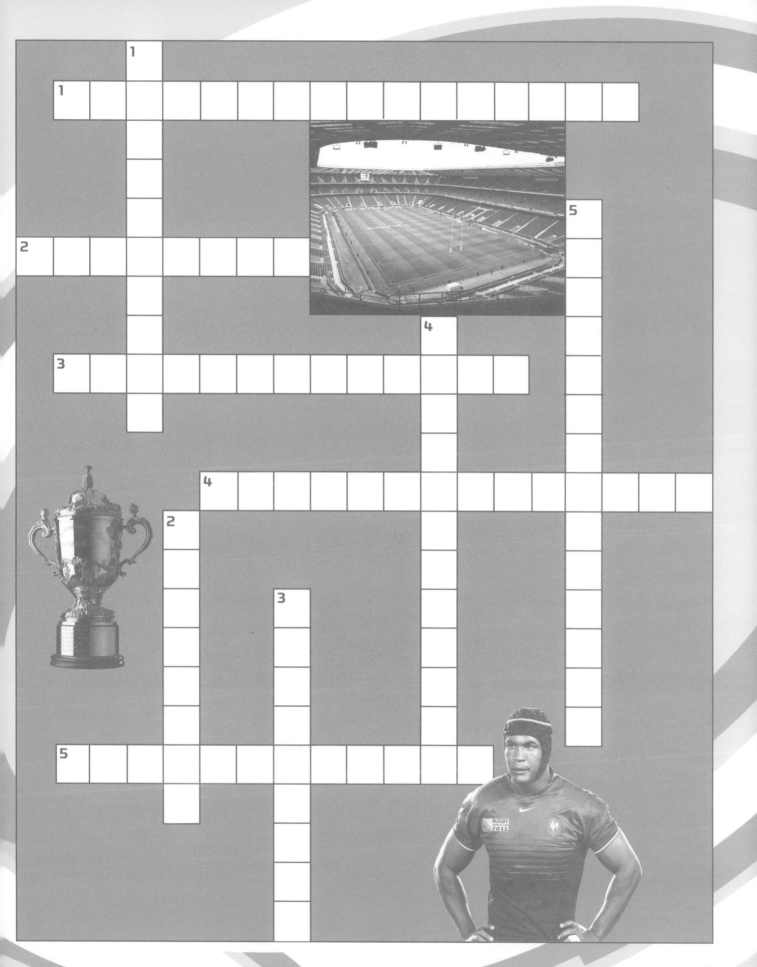

Star players

The world of rugby has many amazing and record-breaking players. Can you guess who these rugby stars are? Fill in their names, find their stickers and place them in the frames.

1

Name: ....

Clues

a. This player helped the England team win RWC 2003.

b. He is the highest-scoring player, with an incredible total of 277 points across four Rugby World Cups.

2

Name: ....

Clues

a. This player is the highest try scorer in Irish history, scoring 45 tries for his country.

b. He is currently the most capped player ever, with 141 caps.

3

Name: ....

Clues

a. This New Zealand captain led his team to victory at Rugby World Cup 2011.

b. He has won IRB Player of the Year a record three times, in 2006, 2009 and 2010.

4

Name: ....

Clues

a. He is the youngest player to score a try on his debut for Wales. He was only 18 years and 214 days old.

b. At RWC 2011 he became the youngest ever try scorer in the history of the Tournament.

The legend

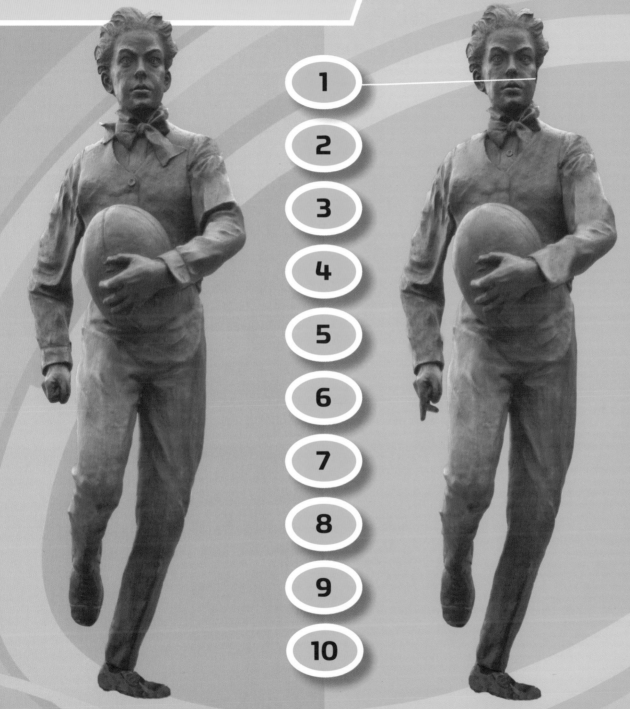

Legend has it that the game of rugby was created when a schoolboy picked up the ball during a football match and started running with it. His name was William Webb Ellis. In tribute to this boy, the Trophy that is awarded to the winning team is called the Webb Ellis Cup.

Ten things have changed from the picture on the left to the picture on the right. Can you spot all the differences? Draw a line from each of the numbers to the thing that has changed. One has been done for you.

Answers on page 56. **37**

Rugby wordsearch

Can you find the following rugby terms in the word search? The words can be read forwards, up, down or diagonally! One has already been done for you.

scrum

turnover

breakdown

ruck

mark

phase

maul

dummy

punt

binding

conversion

touch

try

penalty

tackle

t	a	c	k	l	e	h	v	m	r	v	s	e	v	b
r	s	a	e	w	r	t	u	r	k	t	e	t	n	m
p	u	n	t	s	t	e	m	i	u	t	r	h	a	t
t	i	s	r	s	e	t	v	y	t	c	o	r	c	b
r	p	e	c	c	n	u	m	r	l	k	k	r	w	u
f	h	s	e	r	e	r	v	t	c	l	v	o	h	c
t	a	c	b	u	r	n	k	t	e	o	v	c	m	o
a	s	t	r	m	u	o	w	d	i	w	u	c	u	n
w	e	t	r	o	l	v	c	i	u	o	p	z	w	v
q	w	t	s	k	b	e	t	r	t	m	e	t	l	e
m	a	u	l	e	a	r	w	u	o	w	m	m	b	r
s	d	l	w	u	r	e	y	o	l	m	n	y	t	s
t	b	b	i	n	d	i	n	g	s	e	a	l	l	i
k	p	e	n	a	l	t	y	y	g	l	t	k	o	o
c	h	o	c	d	b	b	r	e	a	k	d	o	w	n

Where in the world?

Twenty countries have qualified for Rugby World Cup 2015. Can you fill in the correct country and pool for each box?

2 Country: ....
Pool: ....

3 Country: ....
Pool: ....

4 Country: ....
Pool: ....

1 Country: ....
Pool: ....

5 Country: ....
Pool: ....

6 Country: ....
Pool: ....

7 Country: ....
Pool: ....

8 Country: ....
Pool: ....

9 Country: ....
Pool: ....

Argentina

Namibia

Australia

New Zealand

Canada

Romania

England

Samoa

Fiji

Scotland

France

South Africa

Georgia

Tonga

Ireland

Uruguay

Italy

USA

Japan

Wales

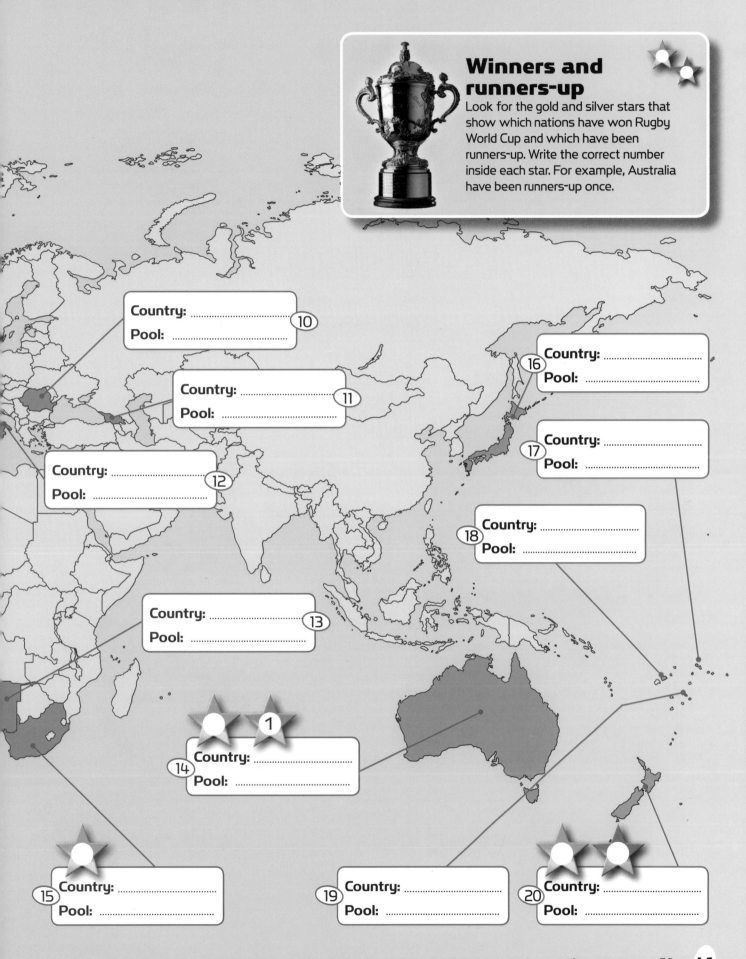

Winners and runners-up

Look for the gold and silver stars that show which nations have won Rugby World Cup and which have been runners-up. Write the correct number inside each star. For example, Australia have been runners-up once.

Country: .... (10)
Pool: ....

Country: .... (11)
Pool: ....

(16) Country: ....
Pool: ....

Country: .... (12)
Pool: ....

(17) Country: ....
Pool: ....

(18) Country: ....
Pool: ....

Country: .... (13)
Pool: ....

(1) Country: ....
(14) Pool: ....

(15) Country: ....
Pool: ....

(19) Country: ....
Pool: ....

(20) Country: ....
Pool: ....

Gilbert MATCH XV

An official rugby ball must be oval and consist of four panels. A rugby ball has been specially designed for Rugby World Cup 2015 and has been named Gilbert MATCH XV.

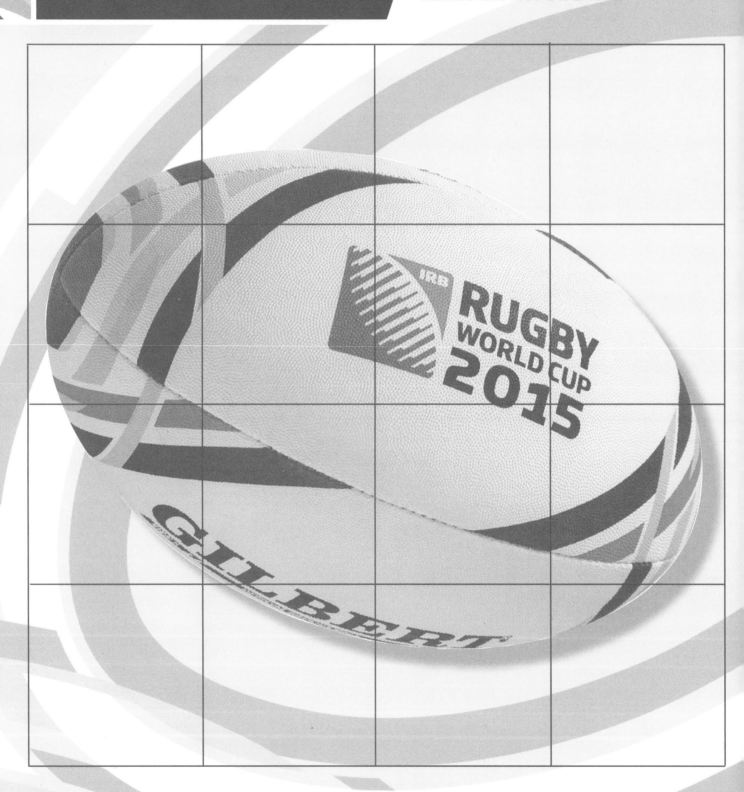

Can you copy the picture of the ball? It might be easier to draw it square by square. Don't forget to colour it in.

Webb Ellis Cup

The Webb Ellis Cup is presented to the winning team at the end of each Rugby World Cup. On the right there are eight copies of the Trophy. All apart from one match the original. Can you find the odd one out?

International Rugby Football Board
The Webb Ellis Cup

1987 NEW ZEALAND
1991 AUSTRALIA
1995 SOUTH AFRICA
1999 AUSTRALIA
2003 ENGLAND
2007 SOUTH AFRICA

FACT CARD 5
Crowning Cup

The two handles of the cup are actually two different characters. At the top of the handle on the left is the head of a satyr. At the top of the handle on the right is the head of a nymph. Amazingly England are the only team in the northern hemisphere to have won the cup. No country has managed to win two Tournaments in a row, yet!

Rugby World Cup: Ultimate quiz

So you think you're a rugby expert? Now it's time to put your knowledge to the test. Read the questions on Rugby World Cup and pick the right answer.

1. How many countries have won Rugby World Cup?

a. ◯ Two
b. ◯ Three
c. ◯ Four
d. ◯ Five

2. Which one of the following countries has not hosted Rugby World Cup?

a. ◯ New Zealand
b. ◯ Italy
c. ◯ France
d. ◯ South Africa

3. How many Rugby World Cups have there been including 2015?

a. ◯ Eight
b. ◯ Five
c. ◯ Seven
d. ◯ Ten

4. Which country is going to host the next Rugby World Cup in 2019?

a. ◯ England
b. ◯ Argentina
c. ◯ Canada
d. ◯ Japan

5. How many stadiums will host rugby matches during RWC 2015?

a. ◯ Ten
b. ◯ Eleven
c. ◯ Thirteen
d. ◯ Fifteen

Answers on page 56.

6. When and where is the first match of RWC 2015?

a. ◯ 19th September at Twickenham Stadium

b. ◯ 18th September at Twickenham Stadium

c. ◯ 19th September at Wembley Stadium

d. ◯ 18th September at Olympic Stadium

7. Who captained the winning team at RWC 2011?

a. ◯ Richie McCaw

b. ◯ Lewis Moody

c. ◯ Dan Carter

d. ◯ Thierry Dusautoir

8. What is the name of the Cup given to RWC winners?

a. ◯ Web Ellis Cup

b. ◯ William Ellis Cup

c. ◯ William Web Ellis Cup

d. ◯ Webb Ellis Cup

9. What has been the biggest winning margin during a RWC match?

a. ◯ 128 points

b. ◯ 142 points

c. ◯ 98 points

d. ◯ 115 points

10. Which stadium will host Rugby World Cup 2015 Final?

a. ◯ Millennium Stadium

b. ◯ Olympic Stadium

c. ◯ Twickenham Stadium

d. ◯ Wembley Stadium

Answers on page 56.

Final fanfare

Five nations have played in seven Rugby World Cup Finals: Australia, England, France, New Zealand and South Africa. Can you answer these tricky questions and fill in the results for all the Finals?

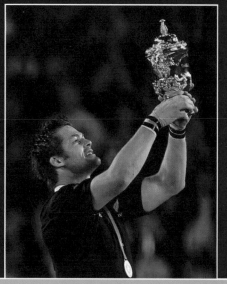

1	France have scored 28 points in their three Finals.
2	The winner's score in 1999 came from two tries, two conversions and seven penalties.
3	Australia have been runners-up once.
4	Only one country from Europe has won Rugby World Cup – in 2003.
5	Australia have scored the most points in Rugby World Cup Finals – 64.
6	In the 2011 Final, the two teams scored two tries, one conversion and one penalty.
7	South Africa have won Rugby World Cup twice, with the same score in each Final.
8	The 1995 Final finished 9-9 at full time. The runners-up scored a penalty in extra time.
9	In both Finals that England finished as runners-up, they scored two penalties.
10	The picture shows the reigning champions. They were also the very first Rugby World Cup winners.

Year	Champions	Result		Runners-up
1987		29		France
1991	Australia	12		England
1995		15		New Zealand
1999	Australia		12	France
2003		20		
2007		15		England
2011			7	France

Answers on page 56.

Final flags

Who do you think will win Rugby World Cup 2015?
Colour in the rectangles with the flags of the
countries you think will come first, second and third.

These are the flags of the countries that qualified for Rugby World Cup 2015.

Argentina Australia Canada England Fiji France Georgia Ireland Italy Japan

Namibia | New Zealand | Romania | Samoa | Scotland | South Africa | Tonga | Uruguay | USA | Wales

Rugby World Cup 2015:
Match schedule

Here is a chart for you to fill in during Rugby World Cup 2015. To help you keep track of all the action, fill in which team has won and lost at each stage of the Tournament and what the final scores are.

	DATE	MATCH NO	MATCH	LOCATION	VENUE	KICK-OFF TIME	SCORE
POOL A	Fri Sept 18	1	England v Fiji	London	Twickenham Stadium	20:00	–
	Sun Sept 20	7	Wales v Uruguay	Cardiff	Millennium Stadium	14:30	–
	Wed Sept 23	10	Australia v Fiji	Cardiff	Millennium Stadium	16:45	–
	Sat Sept 26	16	England v Wales	London	Twickenham Stadium	20:00	–
	Sun Sept 27	17	Australia v Uruguay	Birmingham	Villa Park	12:00	–
	Thurs Oct 1	21	Wales v Fiji	Cardiff	Millennium Stadium	16:45	–
	Sat Oct 3	26	England v Australia	London	Twickenham Stadium	20:00	–
	Tues Oct 6	30	Fiji v Uruguay	Milton Keynes	Stadium MK	20:00	–
	Sat Oct 10	35	Australia v Wales	London	Twickenham Stadium	16:45	–
	Sat Oct 10	36	England v Uruguay	Manchester	Manchester City Stadium	20:00	–
POOL B	Sat Sept 19	4	South Africa v Japan	Brighton	Brighton Community Stadium	16:45	–
	Sun Sept 20	6	Samoa v USA	Brighton	Brighton Community Stadium	12:00	–
	Wed Sept 23	9	Scotland v Japan	Gloucester	Kingsholm Stadium	14:30	–
	Sat Sept 26	15	South Africa v Samoa	Birmingham	Villa Park	16:45	–
	Sun Sept 27	18	Scotland v USA	Leeds	Elland Road	14:30	–
	Sat Oct 3	24	Samoa v Japan	Milton Keynes	Stadium MK	14:30	–
	Sat Oct 3	25	South Africa v Scotland	Newcastle	St James' Park	16:45	–
	Wed Oct 7	31	South Africa v USA	London	Olympic Stadium	16:45	–
	Sat Oct 10	34	Samoa v Scotland	Newcastle	St James' Park	14:30	–
	Sun Oct 11	40	USA v Japan	Gloucester	Kingsholm Stadium	20:00	–
POOL C	Sat Sept 19	2	Tonga v Georgia	Gloucester	Kingsholm Stadium	12:00	–
	Sun Sept 20	8	New Zealand v Argentina	London	Wembley Stadium	16:45	–
	Thurs Sept 24	12	New Zealand v Namibia	London	Olympic Stadium	20:00	–
	Fri Sept 25	13	Argentina v Georgia	Gloucester	Kingsholm Stadium	16:45	–
	Tues Sept 29	20	Tonga v Namibia	Exeter	Sandy Park	16:45	–
	Fri Oct 2	23	New Zealand v Georgia	Cardiff	Millennium Stadium	20:00	–
	Sun Oct 4	27	Argentina v Tonga	Leicester	Leicester City Stadium	14:30	–
	Wed Oct 7	32	Namibia v Georgia	Exeter	Sandy Park	20:00	–
	Fri Oct 9	33	New Zealand v Tonga	Newcastle	St James' Park	20:00	–
	Sun Oct 11	37	Argentina v Namibia	Leicester	Leicester City Stadium	12:00	–

	DATE	MATCH NO	MATCH	LOCATION	VENUE	KICK-OFF TIME	SCORE
POOL D	Sat Sept 19	3	Ireland v Canada	Cardiff	Millennium Stadium	14:30	–
	Sat Sept 19	5	France v Italy	London	Twickenham Stadium	20:00	–
	Wed Sept 23	11	France v Romania	London	Olympic Stadium	20:00	–
	Sat Sept 26	14	Italy v Canada	Leeds	Elland Road	14:30	–
	Sun Sept 27	19	Ireland v Romania	London	Wembley Stadium	16:45	–
	Thurs Oct 1	22	France v Canada	Milton Keynes	Stadium MK	20:00	–
	Sun Oct 4	28	Ireland v Italy	London	Olympic Stadium	16:45	–
	Tues Oct 6	29	Canada v Romania	Leicester	Leicester City Stadium	16:45	–
	Sun Oct 11	38	Italy v Romania	Exeter	Sandy Park	14:30	–
	Sun Oct 11	39	France v Ireland	Cardiff	Millennium Stadium	16:45	–
KNOCKOUT PHASE	Sat Oct 17	41	**Quarter-final 1** Winner (W) Pool B v Runner-Up Pool A v	London	Twickenham Stadium	16:00	–
	Sat Oct 17	42	**Quarter-final 2** Winner Pool C v Runner-Up Pool D v	Cardiff	Millennium Stadium	20:00	–
	Sun Oct 18	43	**Quarter-final 3** Winner Pool D v Runner-Up Pool C v	Cardiff	Millennium Stadium	13:00	–
	Sun Oct 18	44	**Quarter-final 4** Winner Pool A v Runner-Up Pool B v	London	Twickenham Stadium	16:00	–
	Sat Oct 24	45	**Semi-final 1** W Quarter-final 1 v W Quarter-final 2 v	London	Twickenham Stadium	16:00	–
	Sun Oct 25	46	**Semi-final 2** W Quarter-final 3 v W Quarter-final 4 v	London	Twickenham Stadium	16:00	–
	Fri Oct 30	47	**Bronze Final** v	London	Olympic Stadium	20:00	–
FINAL	Sat Oct 31	48	v	London	Twickenham Stadium	16:00	

Have you filled in the latest score?

Rugby World Cup 2015:
The Final

Fill in all the details about the Final – team names, players, substitutes, scorers, man of match etc. Add stickers of the flags for the two teams in the Final.

Saturday, October 31, 2015 • Twickenham • London

V

STARTING XV		
	15	
	14	
	13	
	12	
	11	
	10	
	9	
	1	
	2	
	3	
	4	
	5	
	6	
	7	
	8	

ON THE BENCH		
	16	
	17	
	18	
	19	
	20	
	21	
	22	
	23	

Officials

Referee:

Country:

Assistant Referee 1:

Country:

Assistant Referee 2:

Country:

Final Score

	V	
Points scored by:		Points scored by:

Man of the Match

Name: Position: Team:

Teams' Match Statistics

Tries	First half:		**Tries**	First half:
	Second half:			Second half:
Drop goals	First half:		**Drop goals**	First half:
	Second half:			Second half:
Penalties	First half:		**Penalties**	First half:
	Second half:			Second half:
Scrums	Won:		**Scrums**	Won:
	Lost:			Lost:
	Won opposition's feed:			Won opposition's feed:
Lineouts	Won:		**Lineouts**	Won:
	Lost:			Lost:
	Not straight:			Not straight:
	Won opposition's throw in:			Won opposition's throw in:
Penalty kicks	Scored:		**Penalty kicks**	Scored:
	Missed:			Missed:
Yellow cards:			**Yellow cards:**	
Red cards:			**Red cards:**	
Most memorable moment:			**Most memorable moment:**	

Most memorable moment:

....

....

....

....

....

Most memorable moment:

....

....

....

....

....

Answers

Page 3: a. 2.45pm, b. 3.10pm, c. 3.45pm, d. 4.00pm.

Pages 4–5:
1. Manchester City Stadium, Manchester.
2. Villa Park Stadium, Birmingham.
3. Kingsholm Stadium, Gloucester.
4. Millennium Stadium, Cardiff.
5. Sandy Park Stadium, Exeter.
6. St. James' Park Stadium, Newcastle.
7. Elland Road Stadium, Leeds.
8. Leicester City Stadium, Leicester.
9. Stadium MK, Milton Keynes.
10. Wembley Stadium, London.
11. Olympic Stadium, London.
12. Twickenham Stadium, London.
13. Brighton Community Stadium, Brighton.

Page 6: see right.

Page 7: see right.

Pages 8–9:
2   *Dylan Hartley* – England, Hooker.
14   *Bryan Habana* – South Africa, Wing.
7   *Thierry Dusautoir* – France, Flanker.
3   *Adam Jones* – Wales, Tight-head prop.
15   *Rob Kearney* – Ireland, Full-back.
9   *Will Genia* – Australia, Scrum-half.
10   *Dan Carter* – New Zealand, Fly-half.
4   *Richie Gray* – Scotland, Lock (second row).

Page 11: Maths
1. 920 shirts, 2. 1610 socks (or 805 pairs), 3. 690 shorts.

Pages 12–13: see right.

Page 14: see right.

Page 15:
1. 17, 2. 31, 3. 47, 4. 31, 5. 46. Yes – the answers to 2 and 4 are the same.
Score 3 is the highest.

Page 16: see right.

Page 17:
1. Webb Ellis cup.
2. English rose.
3. Referee whistle.
4. France cockerel.
5. New Zealand flag.

Page 18:
1.d, 2.c, 3.b, 4.a, 5.d, 6.b, 7.d, 8.c, 9.d, 10.a.

Pages 20–21: see right.

Pages 22–23:
1. False – Yes.   2. True – Yes.
3. False – Yes.   4. False – Yes.
5. False – No.   6. True – Yes.
7. False – Yes.   8. False – Yes.
9. False – Yes.   10. True – No.
11. False – Yes.   12. False – Yes.

Pages 24–25: see right.

Pages 26–27:
Pool A – Fiji, Uruguay.
Pool B – Japan, USA.
Pool C – Georgia, Namibia.
Pool D – Canada, Romania.

Pages 28–29: see right.

Page 31:
National anthems:
England – God Save the Queen.
Scotland – Flower of Scotland.
Wales – Hen Wlad Fy Nhadau.
Japan – Kimigayo.
USA – The Star Spangled Banner.
France – La Marseillaise.

Ceremonial dances:
New Zealand – The Haka.
Tonga – The Sipi Tau.
Somoa – The Siva Tau.
Fiji – The Cibi/Bola.

Page 35:
Across:
1.Thierry Dusautoir, 2. John Smit
3. Shane Williams, 4. Jonny Wilkinson, 5. Jason Leonard.

Down:
1. Kieran Read 2. Grant Fox
3. Marc Ellis 4. Jannie De Beer
5. Thretton Palamo.

Page 36:
1. Jonny Wilkinson.
2. Brian O'Driscoll.
3. Richie McCaw.
4. George North.

Page 37: see right.

Page 39: see right.

Pages 40–41:
1. Country: Canada Pool: D,
2. Country: Scotland Pool: B,
3. Country: Ireland Pool: D,
4. Country: Wales Pool: A,
5. Country: USA Pool: B,
6. Country: England Pool: A,
7. Country: France Pool: D,
8. Country: Uruguay Pool: A,
9. Country: Argentina Pool: C,
10. Country: Romania Pool: D,
11. Country: Georgia Pool: C,
12. Country: Italy Pool: D,
13. Country: Namibia Pool: C,
14. Country: Australia Pool: A,
15. Country: South Africa Pool: B,
16. Country: Japan Pool: B,
17. Country: Samoa Pool: B,
18. Country: Fiji Pool: A,
19. Country: Tonga Pool: C,
20. Country: New Zealand Pool: C.

Page 44:
E. *The engraved text is missing from the cup.*

Pages 46–47:
1.c, 2.b, 3.a, 4.d, 5.c, 6.b, 7.a, 8.d, 9.b, 10.c.

Page 48:
1987 New Zealand 29 France 9.
1991 Australia 12 England 6.
1995 South Africa 15 New Zealand 12.
1999 Australia 35 France 12.
2003 England 20 Australia 17.
2007 South Africa 15 England 6.
2011 New Zealand 8 France 7.

4-5

12-13

16

7

1	2	3	4	5
6	7	8	9	10
11	12	13	14	15

17

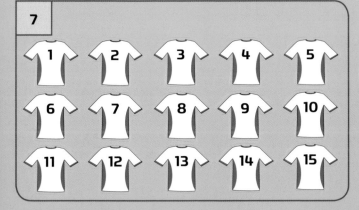

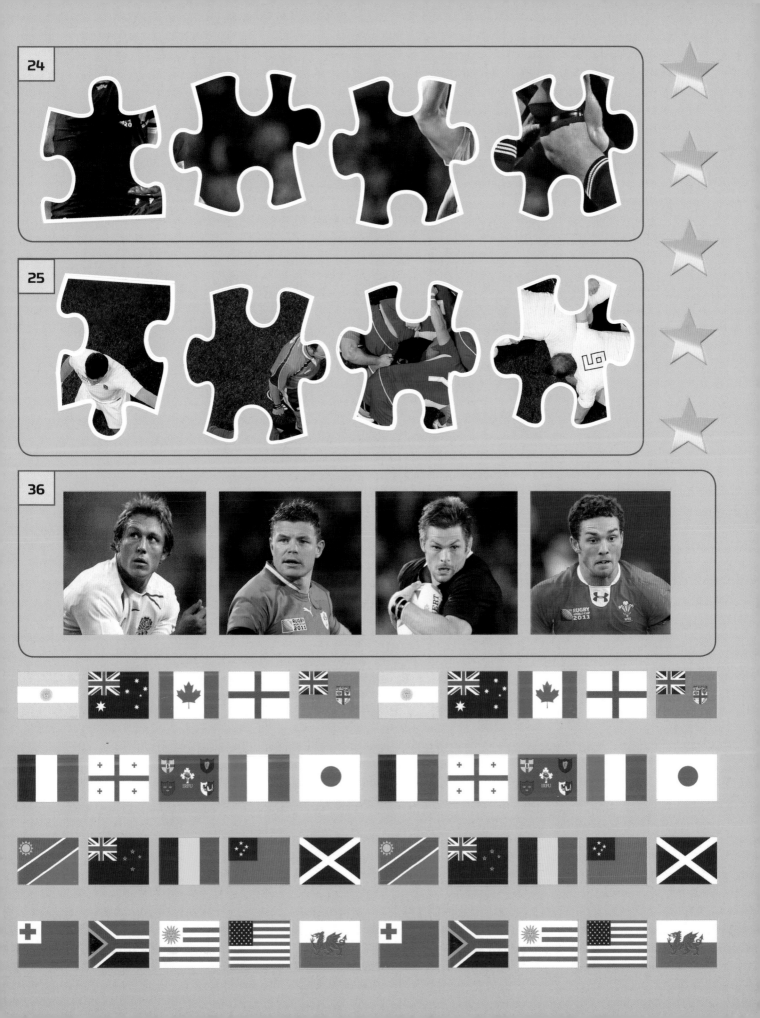